W9-AVL-882

HOW DID THEY BUILD THAT?
BRIDGE

BY VICKY FRANCHINO

COMMUNITY·CONNECTIONS

CHERRY LAKE
Publishing

Published in the United States of America by Cherry Lake Publishing
Ann Arbor, Michigan
www.cherrylakepublishing.com

Content Adviser: Nancy Kristof
Reading Adviser: Cecilia Minden-Cupp, PhD, Literacy Consultant

Photo Credits: Cover, pages 1 and 11, ©Brandon Holmes, used under license from Shutterstock, Inc.; page 5, ©Steve Lovegrove, used under license from Shutterstock, Inc.; page 7, ©Dendron/Dreamstime.com; page 9, ©Fedor Selivanov, used under license from Shutterstock, Inc.; page 13, ©Vladimir Mucibabic, used under license from Shutterstock, Inc.; page 15, ©iStockphoto.com/LawrenceSawyer; page 17, ©kai hecker, used under license from Shutterstock, Inc.; page 19, ©Iain Masterton/Alamy; page 21, ©Brandon Seidel, used under license from Shutterstock, Inc.

LIBRARY OF CONGRESS CATALOGING-IN-PUBLICATION DATA
Franchino, Vicky.
  How did they build that? Bridge / by Vicky Franchino.
    p. cm.—(Community connections)
Includes index.
ISBN-13: 978-1-60279-483-2
ISBN-10: 1-60279-483-9
1. Bridges—Juvenile literature. I. Title. II. Title: Bridge. III. Series.
TG148.F73 2009
624.2—dc22   2008046616

Cherry Lake Publishing would like to acknowledge the work of The Partnership for 21st Century Skills. Please visit www.21stcenturyskills.org for more information.

BRIDGE

CONTENTS

HOW DID THEY BUILD THAT?

HOW DO BRIDGES HELP US?

A bridge helps us get from one place to another. A bridge can go over land or water. Sometimes they go over roads and train tracks. Big bridges go over rivers. Do you know how bridges are made? Let's learn more about bridges.

The Sydney Harbor Bridge is in Australia.

Some bridges are small. Others are large. Many old bridges were made of wood and stone. Today, bridges are often made of concrete and steel. These are very strong materials. They will last for a long time.

Some bridges are just big enough for people to walk on.

Look for different types of bridges near your house. Do any of the bridges have interesting designs? Are all of them for cars? Sometimes you might find a bridge in a surprising place. Look in a park or a garden.

TYPES OF BRIDGES

A beam bridge is often a simple bridge. It is held up by the ground or by strong supports called **piers**. Beam bridges are often made for people to walk over.

Drawbridges are bridges that lift up to let large boats pass through. These bridges lower again to let cars or people cross over the water.

Tower Bridge in London is a famous drawbridge.

Some of the most famous bridges are **suspension bridges**. Strong **cables** hold them up. The cables are attached to towers and to blocks called **anchorages**. The towers and anchorages keep the bridge from falling.

One well-known suspension bridge is the Golden Gate Bridge in San Francisco.

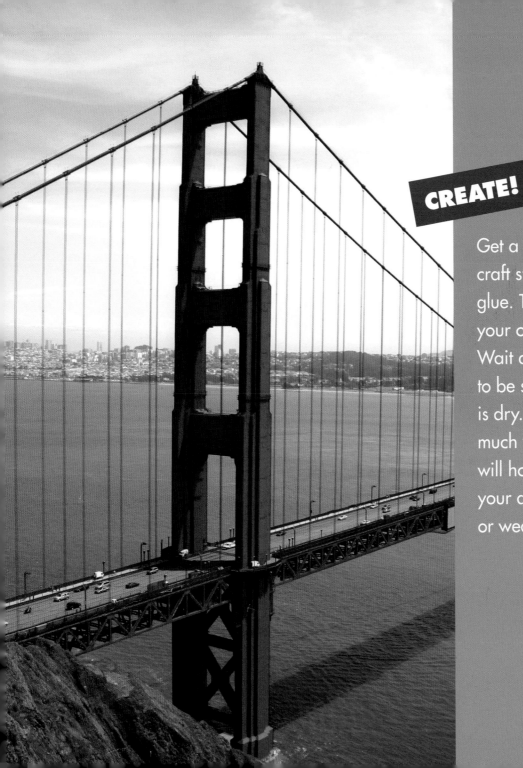

Get a box of wooden craft sticks and some glue. Try building your own bridge. Wait a day or two to be sure the glue is dry. Then see how much your bridge will hold. Was your design strong or weak?

11

GETTING READY TO BUILD

City planners figure out how many people and cars will use a bridge.

An **engineer** decides what type of bridge will work best. Sometimes engineers work with **architects** to design bridges. Architects often help decide what the bridge will look like.

Building a bridge takes careful planning.

Engineers make sure the bridge will be strong. They learn about wind and earthquakes. They find out how heavy the bridge will be. Engineers decide what the bridge will be made of. They decide how the pieces will go together.

In 2007, a bridge in Minneapolis collapsed because it was not built correctly.

Inspectors are important members of the bridge building team. They make sure everyone's work is done right. Why do you think it is important for someone to check the work before a bridge is used?

BUILDING THE BRIDGE

Construction begins with the base. Then the piers are built. If the piers are in water, workers might use a **caisson**. Caissons sit on the bottom of the lake or river. They stick out of the water. Workers go inside to build the part of the bridge that is underwater.

The Brooklyn Bridge in New York was built using caissons.

A beam bridge is usually made of pieces of concrete and steel. Workers use cranes to lift the pieces into the right place.

For an **arch** bridge, workers start on both sides. They work toward the middle. The arch will not be strong until the two sides come together. Cables or **scaffolds** hold up the pieces while people are working.

This picture was taken when Lupu Bridge in China was being built. It is the longest steel arch bridge in the world.

The towers of suspension bridges are built first. Then workers add cables that are made of many wires. When the cables are in place, they can support the deck. That is the part of the bridge you drive or walk on. Then workers can pave the roadway. They add lights. Finally, the bridge is painted.

Now the bridge is ready for travelers. Enjoy the trip!

Many cars travel across bridges every day.

GLOSSARY

anchorages (ANG-kur-ij-iz) heavy blocks of concrete that the cables of a suspension bridge are attached to

arch (ARCH) a curved structure that often helps support a bridge or building

architects (AR-ki-tektss) people who design bridges and other structures

cables (KAY-buhlz) thick wires or ropes

caisson (KAY-sahn) an underwater chamber that people work in while building a bridge

engineer (en-juh-NIHR) a person who helps to plan and build a bridge

piers (PIHRZ) strong supports for bridges

scaffolds (SKAF-uhlds) structures that hold up part of a bridge or other building while it's being built

suspension bridges (suh-SPEN-shun BRIJ-es) bridges that are hung from cables attached to towers

FIND OUT MORE

BOOKS

Simon, Seymour. *Bridges*. San Francisco: SeaStar Books, 2005.

Tieck, Sarah. *Brooklyn Bridge*. Edina, MN: ABDO Publishing Company, 2008.

WEB SITES

Building Big: Bridge Basics
www.pbs.org/wgbh/buildingbig/bridge/basics.html
Learn more about how different kinds of bridges are built

Science Rocks! Suspension Bridge
pbskids.org/zoom/activities/sci/suspensionbridge.html
Try out this fun activity and build your own suspension bridge

INDEX

ABOUT THE AUTHOR

Vicky Franchino has crossed some of the most interesting bridges in the United States including the Brooklyn Bridge (where you can walk *above* the cars!) and the Golden Gate Bridge. Vicky lives with her husband and three daughters in Madison, Wisconsin.